100 Must Do

THAILAND

Outdoor Adventures, TOP 10 Beaches, Phuket, Eat & Drink, Historical and Cultural Sights, Advice of Local people, Souvenirs

by Kevin Hampton

Copyright 2018 by Kevin Hampton - All rights reserved.

All rights Reserved. No part of this publication or the information in it may be quoted from or reproduced in any form by means such as printing, scanning, photocopying or otherwise without prior written permission of the copyright holder.

Disclaimer and Terms of Use: Effort has been made to ensure that the information in this book is accurate and complete, however, the author and the publisher do not warrant the accuracy of the information, text, and graphics contained within the book due to the rapidly changing nature of science, research, known and unknown facts and the internet. The Author and the publisher do not hold any responsibility for errors, omissions or contrary interpretation of the subject matter herein. This book is presented solely for motivational and informational purposes only.

Table of Contents

Introduction 4

Historical and Cultural Sights 6

Festivals Calendar 18

Unusual and Interesting Places 21

Outdoor Adventures and Nature 28

TOP 10 Beaches 35

Eat and Drink 41

TOP 10 Party Bars and Clubs 46

Original Local/Authentic Souvenirs 50

Introduction

Thailand (or Kingdom of Thailand) is located in Southeast Asia. It has a total area of approximately 513,000 km2 (198,000 sq mi), it is the world's 50th-largest country and has around a population of 66 million making it the20th-most-populous country in the world.

The frontiers of Thailand includes Myanmar and Laos to the north, Laos and Cambodia to the east, the Gulf of Thailand and Malaysia to the south, and the Andaman Sea and the southern extremity of Myanmar to the west.

The capital city is Bangkok and it is the most populous city in the country. The currency of Thailand is called a baht .The politics of Thailand is currently conducted within the framework of a constitutional monarchy.

Thailand comprises several distinct geographic regions. The north of the country is the mountainous area of the Thai highlands. The highest point is the Doi Inthanon situated in the Thanon Thong Chai Range , which is almost at 2,565 meters (8,415 ft) above sea level. The northeast, Isan, consists of the Khorat Plateau, which is bordered by the Mekong River in the east. The center of the country is flat and dominated by the Chao Phraya river valley, which in turn runs into the Gulf of Thailand.

The south of Thailand consists of the narrow Kra Isthmus that widens into the Malay Peninsula. The Chao Phraya and the Mekong River are the main water courses of rural Thailand. The Gulf of Thailand covers 320,000 square kilometers and is fed by the Chao Phraya, Mae Klong, Bang Pakong, and Tapi Rivers. This is a major attraction to the tourism sector because of its clear shallow waters along the coasts in the southern region and the Kra Isthmus. Whereas the eastern shore of the Gulf of Thailand is an industrial centre of Thailand which consists of the kingdom's premier deep water port in Sattahip and its busiest commercial port named Laem Chabang. Places Phuket, Krabi, Ranong, Phang Nga and Trang, and their islands, all lay along the coasts of the Andaman Sea and, they are a tourist magnet for visitors from around the world.

The climate is mainly influenced by monsoon winds that have a seasonal character (the southwest and northeast monsoon). The southwest monsoon, starts from May, last until October, and is characterized by movement of warm, moist air from the Indian Ocean to Thailand, causing abundant rainfall over most of the country. Whereas the northeast monsoon starts from October and lasts until February and brings the cold and dry air from China to most parts of Thailand. In the southern part of Thailand, the northeast monsoon brings mild weather and abundant rainfall on the eastern coast of that region. Most of the areas of Thailand has a "tropical wet and dry or savanna climate" type whereas the south and the eastern tip of the east have a tropical monsoon climate.

Based on these facts the seasons of Thailand can be put into three categories. The rainy or southwest monsoon season (mid–May to mid–October) this prevails over most of the country. This is characterized by abundant rain with August and September being the wettest period of *the year, which can even occasionally lead to floods. Winter or the northeast monsoon starts from mid–October and lasts until mid–February. Most of Thailand experiences dry weather during this season with mild temperatures. Summer or the pre–monsoon season runs from mid–February until mid–May and is characterized by warmer weather present throughout the country.*

Because of its diverse geographical features and favorable climatic conditions Thailand has many places of attraction, which includes world class beaches in the south, the mountainous areas along the north the bustling cities like Bangkok and Chiang Maii and the biodiversity which mostly consists of elephants and monkeys.

Historical and Cultural Sights

Thailand is one of the countries that has stunning features. Thailand has various historical and cultural sights that attract tourists. It also has shrines, temples, ruins, and historic architecture sites that are very fine-looking.

Sai Yok national park

Location: Sai Yok, Sai Yok District, Kanchanaburi 71150

It covers almost 958 km² in Sai Yok District of Kanchanaburi Province, which is located 100 km northwest of Kanchanaburi City. The Sai Yok National Park is part of the Western Forex Complex which covers almost 18,730 km² and consists of 19 protected sites between Myanmar and Thailand. The park is popular for its waterfalls, caves, historical sites and raft houses along the River Kwai.

Dry evergreen forest with bamboo and other trees cover the mountain region. It has the highest elevation of 1328 meters which is near to the Myanmar border. During the Japanese occupation majority of the area was deforested, however this area was replanted later.

Hellfire Pass & Memorial Museum

Location: Tha Sao, Sai Yok District, Kanchanaburi 71150

The museum is located on Highway which is about 80 km outside Kanchanaburi. It is a 500 m-long portion of rock that was dug out by thousand prisoners of war. They used this rock to pave the way for the Death Railway. Among the prisoners almost seven hundred men died during the 12 long work period. One can walk to the old railway track into the jungle which almost takes about 4 to 5 hours and visit the memorial museum honoring those who were killed in the process of construction. The museum has artifacts, tools, and photos from that period.

The National Museum Bangkok

Location: Na Phra That Alley, Khwaeng Phra Borom Maha Ratchawang, Khet Phra Nakhon, Krung Thep Maha Nakhon 10200

National Museum Bangkok has different buildings that have royal barges, furniture, and art of which they originated from different kingdoms of Thailand. The museum has many Thai artifacts. The museum building is divided according to the type of handicrafts, and archaeology. In 1934 it was lounged as a national museum, and it has always attracted many visitors up to date.

Chiang Mai National Museum

Location: 451 หมู่ 2 ถนน ซุปเปอร์ไฮเวย์ เชียงใหม่-ลำปาง Tambon Chang Phueak, Amphoe Mueang Chiang Mai, Chang Wat Chiang Mai 50000

Chiang Mai National Museum is a relatively small museum in Thailand. It is fully packed with Lanna style artifacts such as ceramics, handicrafts, arts, and more. It usually has the information of economic development of the city and education background. The Chiang Mai National Museum is generally opened on Sundays and Monday as from 9 am to 4 pm; visitors are urged to come and explore the history of Thailand.

Thai-Burma Railway Centre Museum

Location: 73 Chao Khun Nen Rd, Ban Nuea, Amphoe Mueang Kanchanaburi, Chang Wat Kanchanaburi 71000

The Thai Burma Railway was constructed by prisoners during the world war II. It was famously recognized as Death Railway since the building of its tracts resulted in too many deaths of prisoners. Prisoners faced with harsh conditions such as diseases infection, hunger, and the harsh rule of Japanese captors. The Museum always educate people on the history of the Railway's existence by the thoughtful and interactive way to make understanding to be easier. The museum is always open daily, and it's affordable to pay admission fee upon entrance.

Jeath War Museum

Location: Ban Tai, Mueang Kanchanaburi District, Kanchanaburi 71000

Its name originates from those countries that were involved in the war: Japan, England, America, Thailand, and Holland.

The museum is designed to be an exact replica of an actual prisoner of war camp. It is located on the grounds of Wat Chai Chumphon, and is maintained by a monk and allows travelers a look at the harsh realities of life within these camps. The museum bunks, photographs, and other authentic items, which resembles the ones, present at the time of war. The display also includes written accounts from actual prisoners of war, their family members, and authors who interviewed POWs.

Erawan National Park

Location: Tha Kradan, Si Sawat District, Kanchanaburi 71250

Erawan is a mythical creature, a white elephant. The park is named after this creature on 1975. This park is open from 7 am to 4:30 pm every day. This is a best-known natural attraction in Kanchanaburi. It consists of a seven-tiered Erawan Falls. It is located 65 km from Kanchanaburi. The water runs down the mountains which are surrounded by lush vegetation and the Limestone Mountains. There are many unique creatures including elephants, gibbons and king cobras. There are four major caves in the park these caves have ancient paintings.

Tiger Kingdom

Location: 51/1 หมู่ที่ 7 ถนน แม่ริม - สะเมิง Rim Tai, Amphoe Mae Rim, Chang Wat Chiang Mai 50180

This is a zoo that provides people with an opportunity to interact with animals. Located 15 km away from Chiang Mai city the place is famous for its tigers. The entry fee is 600 to 1200 baht per person. If you want to get close to tigers and snap a picture this is the place to go.

Chiang Mai City Arts & Cultural Centre

Location: Prapokkloa Rd, Tambon Si Phum, Amphoe Mueang Chiang Mai, Chang Wat Chiang Mai 50200

Situated in the Prapokklao Rd, between Rajdumnern Rd, the museum is open from 8.00 am to 5.00 pm. This is a fully modernized multimedia center. The events in history are organized in chronological order. People can watch a multimedia presentation on specific topics of their choice. The entry fee is 90 baht.

Art in Paradise

Location: 78/34หมู่ที่ 9 Pattayasaisong Rd, Bang Lamung District, Chon Buri 20150

Art in paradise is located on Changklan Rd. This is an illusion art museum, which offers a service to take photos in "3D" scenes. This is favorite location for a family as well as other crowds. The entry fee is 300 baht for adults and 200 baht for children.

Three Kingdoms Theme Park

Location: เลข ที่100 9 เลขที่154 Pong, Bang Lamung District, Chon Buri 20150

A Chinese styled theme park based on Chinese legends. The entry fee is 150 baht per adult and 80 baht for children.

Sanctuary of Truth

Location: 206/2 หมู่ที่5 Na Kluea 12 Alley, Muang Pattaya, Amphoe Bang Lamung, Chang Wat Chon Buri 20150

This is a temple made of wood situated by the sea at Laem Ratchawet, North Pattaya. The construction was started in 1981, it is still an unfinished project this depicts the philosophical and spiritual growth of civilization. The entrance fee is 50 Bahts.

Million year Stone Park and crocodile farm

Location: 22/1 หมู่ที่1 Nong Pla Lai, Amphoe Bang Lamung, Chang Wat Chon Buri 20150

As the name suggests this is a zoo. Many rare and exotic animals are kept in the place. They conduct magic shows animal shows and crocodile shows regularly. The entrance fee is 300 baht for adults and 150 baht for children.

Cartoon Network Amusement Park

Location: 888 Moo8 NaJomtien Najomtien, Sattahip District, Chon Buri 20250

This is one among the major attraction of the Pattaya. Many cartoon network characters are on display here. People can take photos with their favorite cartoon network characters. The entry fee is 1590 baht per person.

The grand palace

Location: 1 Na Phra Lan Rd, Khwaeng Phra Borom Maha Ratchawang, Khet Phra Nakhon, Krung Thep Maha Nakhon 10200

The grand palace is the formal residence of the royals. it was built by King Rama I laid the foundation stone for the palace after moving his capital city to Bangkok in 1782. It is believed that bricks from the ruins of royal palace, forts and walls in Ayutthaya were used to construct this palace. The bricks were transported to Bangkok from Ayutthaya on water. The royal family no more stays in the palace.

The palace is roughly rectangular and it occupies a combined area of 218,400 square meters, surrounded by four walls. It is located alonng the banks of Chao Phraya River in the Phra Nakhon District.

The palace includes many buildings, which were created by successive kings during their time of regime. Though the Grand Palace is open to the public as a museum it is still used by several royal offices situated inside. During the time of monarchy this place served as the administrative and religious center. The palace was considered as a city within the city where special palace rules and laws were in place to manage the affairs within the palace. In the early 1900s, the kings built several palaces elsewhere and moved out to those palaces. Today the grand palace is the center of several royal ceremonies. The Grand Palace also has a front palace, which was occupied by the deputy king of the monarchy. This position was abolished by King Rama V

Lumphini Park

Location: Rama IV Rd, Khwaeng Lumphini, Khet Pathum Wan, Krung Thep Maha Nakhon 10330

Lumphini Park is another attraction in the city. The place was designed to host the Thai craft and flowers. People can go boating and trekking in the area. At times they host concerts in the park.

Wat Phra Kaew - Temple of the Emerald Buddha

Location: Na Phra Lan Rd, Khwaeng Phra Borom Maha Ratchawang, Khet Phra Nakhon, Krung Thep Maha Nakhon 10200

The Emerald Buddha is the holiest relic in Thai Buddhism, and may only be approached by the King. The statue has three different golden "outfits" corresponding to the Thai seasons (hot, dry, and monsoon), and are changed thrice annually in a special ceremony.

The Emerald Buddha is is about 66 centimeters tall and a dark green statue which. It is carved out from a single jade stone. The legend has it that the statue was first made by sage in called Nagasena in Patna, India during 43 BC. The statue is believed to bring prosperity to a country and legitimacy to the leader who is ruling the country. From India it was shifted to Sri Lanka. Burmese requested the statue so the statue was loaded on a ship but the ship never made it to Burma. Then the Statue was found in Cambodia from where it was taken to Ayutthaya by the conquerors. There are evidences of the statues wear about in history from the 1300s. In 1546 the Vietnamese got hold of the Emerald Buddha. and it remained in Vietnam for 218 years. Later King Ram I took it back to Bangkok. The Wat Phra Kaew has old Bangkok style of architecture. It is famous for the decorations and monuments. The temple follows strict rules for dress code. Visitors can rent appropriate dress at the temple entrance. Men have to wear long trousers and sleeved shirts and shoes. Women are to wear long skirts.

Get away from the crowds and explore the outer areas of the temple. Especially notice the beautiful fresco murals on the outer walls, depicting scenes from Hindu-Buddhist mythology.

It's a good idea to arrive at the temple early; it can get very hot and very crowded fast!

Wat Pho - Temple of the Reclining Buddha

Location: 2 Sanam Chai Rd, Khwaeng Phra Borom Maha Ratchawang, Khet Phra Nakhon, Krung Thep Maha Nakhon 10200

Referenced by Murray Head (...muddy old river or Reclining Buddha...), Wat Pho may be, after Wat Phra Kaew, the most famous temple in Bangkok.

The image of the Reclining Buddha depicts the peaceful death of Siddharta Gautama (The Buddha) as he prepares to enter Nirvana. Pay special attention to the feet of the Buddha, which are inlaid with intricate mother-of-pearl images.

Entry for foreigners only costs 50 baht, making it much more affordable to visit on a budget than Wat Phra Kaew.

The dress code is strictly enforced at Wat Pho. Anyone who is inappropriately dressed (short skirts or sleeveless shirts for men or women) will be forced to rent an ugly lime green bathrobe-type-thing. I don't know how often those are washed... Show respect to the Thai culture and dress appropriately when visiting a temple.

Wander around the temple grounds to explore the colorful stupas reminiscent of a magical Candyland.

Wat Arun - Temple of the Dawn

Location: 158 Thanon Wang Doem, Khwaeng Wat Arun, Khet Bangkok Yai, Krung Thep Maha Nakhon 10600

Across the river from Wat Phra Kaew and Wat Pho sits Wat Arun, the Temple of the Dawn, and one of the most iconic landmarks to stand out on Bangkok's skyline.

Named for the Hindu god Vishnu, the personification of the sun, Wat Arun lies on the western side of the river. Despite its name, it's actually best viewed at sunset, when the sky behind it is lit up fiery orange and red.

The main Khmer-style spire is inlaid with tiles made of broken porcelain pottery. Visitors have a chance to climb the steep steps to get to the upper level for nice views across the river.

Wat Benchamabophit - The Marble Temple

Location: 69 Thanon Si Ayutthaya, Khwaeng Dusit, Khet Dusit, Krung Thep Maha Nakhon 10300

Look at the back of a Thai five-baht coin to see the main wat of the beautiful Marble Temple.

Built of Italian marble and incorporating beautiful stained-glass windows, the Marble Temple was constructed according to the specifications of the Thai king in 1911.

With its steep eaves, pillars, and lion statues, the Marble Temple is the image of the quintessential Thai temple, and one of the most beautiful in Bangkok. It's more peaceful and less crowded than Wat Pho, Wat Arun, and Wat Phra Kaew.

Explore the temple's quiet gardens, buy some bread to feed the koi, and enjoy the peaceful atmosphere at this temple which exemplifies Bangkok-era Thai temple architecture.

Wat Phra Si Sanphet

Location: Pratuchai, Phra Nakhon Si Ayutthaya District, Phra Nakhon Si Ayutthaya 13000

This temple is located at Sri Sanphet Rd. and remains open from 8.00 am to 6.00 pm every day. The cost of entry is 50 Baht. This is the largest temple in Ayutthaya. The main attraction of the temple is the restored Stupas or pillar-like structures. This is located in the royal ground and only the royal religious ceremonies were held here.

Viharn Phra Mongkol Bopit

Location: นเรศวร ประตูชัย Naresuan Rd, Tambon Pratuchai, Amphoe Phra Nakhon Si Ayutthaya, Chang Wat Phra Nakhon Si Ayutthaya 13000

Is located at Sri Sanphet Rd. This is a beautiful building that houses a large bronze image of Buddha. Though it was destroyed during the Burmese invasion many of parts were renovated recently Royal ceremony took place in the area.

Ayutthaya Historical Study Centre

Location: Pratuchai, Phra Nakhon Si Ayutthaya District, Phra Nakhon Si Ayutthaya 13000

Ayutthaya Historical Study Centre, Rojana Rd (Rotchana Rd), has many artefacts about the history of Ayutthaya. It mainly focuses on the relationship of the city with other parts of the world. The entrance fee is 100 baht for adults and 50 Baths for children.

Wat Saket - The Golden Mount

Location: ถนน บริพัตร Khwaeng Ban Bat, Khet Pom Prap Sattru Phai, Krung Thep Maha Nakhon 10100

One of the best experiences in Bangkok is visiting the Golden Mount at Wat Saket. One of the most stunning historic temples in Bangkok's Old Town, the Golden Mount is unlike any other temple in the city. The main stupa is at the top of a hill overlooking the city. Wind your way up the cool jungle path to the top of the temple, ringing prayer bells along the way.

The top of the temple has one of the best 360 views in all of Bangkok. Bells jingle and prayer flags crack in the breeze as worshipers circle the main golden stupa offering prayers.

There is also a coffee shop about halfway up. Grab an ice-cold Thai tea and enjoy the relaxing and beautiful atmosphere of one of Bangkok's best temples. Entry is only 20 baht per person - an excellent deal for this fun and holy experience. You can reach this temple by taking the famous river canal boats.

Wat Chiang Man

Location: 71 Ratchapakhinai Rd, ตำบล ศรีภูมิ Amphoe Mueang Chiang Mai, Chang Wat Chiang Mai 50200

Wat Chiang Man located in Rajpakinai Rd. is the oldest royal temple Chiang Man. It was founded in 1296 the Buddha images framed here is 1800 to 25000 year old. King Mengrai lived here while the city was being constructed. PraSeh-Taang Kamaneeee, a crystal kept in the temple believed to have the power to bring rain.

Wat Phrathat Doi Suthep

Location: 9 หมู่9 ต.สุเทพ อ.เมืองเชียงใหม่ Chang Wat Chiang Mai 50200

Build in 1383 the temple is situated 1,073 meters elevation on Mount Suthep, which is around 18 km from the city. The legend says that an elephant pocked the spot for the temple. A white elephant was left to roam around the jungle upon reaching a specific spot it trumpeted circled around three times and knell down and died. This space was identified for the temple. One has to climb over 300 steps to reach the temple. The steps are decorated with colorful drawings of dragons (naga). The temple has a series of bells which devotees are to ring as a part of their custom. The temple is plated in gold. Devotees circle around the temple for blessings for the god. And one can have a beautiful view of the city from the top of the temple.

Chantharakasem National Museum

Location: Hua Ro, Phra Nakhon Si Ayutthaya District, Phra Nakhon Si Ayutthaya 13000

Chantharakasem National Museum on Uthong Rd is another attraction in the area it was constructed in 1577 by King Naresuan the Great.

Chao Sam Phraya National Museum

Location: 108 โรจนะ ถนน เทศบาลเมืองอโยธยา ตำบลประตูชัย Amphoe Phra Nakhon Si Ayutthaya, Chang Wat Phra Nakhon Si Ayutthaya 13000

The surveying treasures of Aytthayawas has been collected and put in this Museum for display. The entry fee is 150 bahts.

Festivals Calendar

Kek River Rafting Festival

Date: July and October

It's the most enjoyed activity since Kek River is rafting along of eight-kilometer distance. It takes about 2 to 4 hours depending on the water level. The most challenging stage is stage1 to stage 5 because the river is quite harsh and rough rafting course. You are advised to be very cautiously and always pay attention to the instruction of the officers. This event is conducted at Phitsanulok in July and October.

Kaeng Hin Phoeng Whitewater Rafting Festival

Date: June and October

This festival is carried out per annum especially June and October. During this period the water level is always high, providing a platform for faster flow, cleaner rapid and less dangerous conditions. During the event, there is still a rafting competition at Kaeng Hin Phoeng.

Bangkok's International Festival of Dance and Music

Date: September to October

Bangkok's International Festival of Dance and Music is undoubtedly a celebrity surprise-filled programmed that spans the whole range of genres. It's an occasion that always reaffirms Bangkok's place as a traditional city. There are various fantastic activities conducted such as classical concerts, operas, classical ballets, and folk dances. The event is carried out in Thailand cultural center at Bangkok on 12th September to 18th October yearly. The tickets range from USD 15 to 90. People from around the world come to join the festival.

Kluai Khai Fair

Date: September

Kluai Khai is well-known as a product of this region, so The Kluai Khai Fair is conducted in September every year to encourage the local people to eat bananas. There are banana competitions held on the making of Krayasat which is a local sweet banana. There is always entertainment activities for people to enjoy.

Chinese New Year

Date: January and February

Chinese New Year is called drut jeen, Thais with Chinese ancestry celebrate New Year based on the lunar calendar every year. Over 14 percent of people in Thailand have chines origin. Though this festival is celebrated across Thailand, certain places such as China town in Bangkok, where a high number of Chinese Thais live, celebrates this in a grand manner. The Odeon Gate at Bangkok is the official centre for the celebrations. This event falls during the months of January and February every year. This is a family festival where everyone gets involved in house cleaning and fireworks. In certain cities public events and celebrations are also held.

Makha Bucha

Date: February or March

Makha Bucha is one of three holy days marking important moments of Buddha's life, Makha Bucha or Magha Puja falls on the full moon of the third lunar month. This festival is held to commemorate Buddha preaching to his disciples/Sangha of enlightened monks who came to hear him on the same day without sending them a word. This is a public holiday where people visit temples. They observe five precepts by abstaining from killing, stealing, lying, consuming alcohol and sexual misconducts. People join monks to celebrate this day. Monks are offered food. At the end of the day people join the Candle Light Procession which is held by all temples. Bars in the country remain closed during this day. This festival falls in the month of February or March.

Songkran Festival

Date: 12th to 14th April

Songkran is the Thai New Year. This is observed every year 12th to 14th of April. The root of the word Songkran is Sankranti, which means astrological passage. This has a close relationship with Maka Sankranti, a Hindu festival celebrated in India to mark the beginning of spring. The morning of the New Year begins with visiting temples and prayers. The monks are offered food. Then as tradition, water is poured onto the statues of Buddha. This symbolically means washing away the sins and bad luck. The elders are treated with respect during the festival. Youngsters pour water on to the hands of elders to show reverence. All the roads are closed on the day. Roads are used for water fights and celebrations. People come to the street with water guns and splash water on each other. Everyone is targeted whether they are willing or unwilling for the fight.

Unusual and Interesting Places

Yala

Yala is a university town and the cleanest city in Thailand. The biggest attraction here is Wat Kuha Pi Muk or Cave-front Temple. This Srivijaya-period cave temple features a reclining Buddha that dates back to AD 757. The city is famous for seafood restaurants.

Pattai

Pattai has a rich tradition, it also has some of the best beaches in the country. Several families have set up beachfront restaurants in the area. The food in the area is very different for the food from another part of Thailand.

Floating markets

The major attraction is floating markets, where the sellers come to the market on their boats and sell their stuff. This is a major tourist attraction. Khlong Lat Mayom and Thaling Chan are the two most popular floating markets in the city.

Chatuchak Market

The Chatuchak Market is one of the biggest markets in the country. It is held on weekends. It covers more than one kilometer with 15,000 booths selling almost anything from every corner of Thailand. This market has been active in Bangkok for decades. The market draws in more than 200,000 customers a day. This market attracts foreigners as well as tourist. The market has 27 sections that sell handicrafts, wooden furniture, ceramic wares, paintings, dolls, accessories, jewelry and many other such things at low price. There are plenty of restaurants and small cafes to dine. The sellers are also ready to ship your items back to your place for a price. The market is open on Sundays and Saturdays from 6.00 am to 6.00 pm a Sky train to Mo Chit station is the easiest and cheapest way to get to this area.

Chao Phrom Market

It is Located at Pasak River near U-Thong Rd. Food, clothing, and day to day supplies are offered in the shops of this market. There are several markets opened at night with many street hawkers selling food, electronics and clothes.

Pak KlongTalat Flower Market

The flower market brings flowers from all over Thailand. Though it is open 24 hours a day it is busy during the early evening hours. The market has a long history it was started in 1782 as a fluting market later it evolved into the market that you can find today. The market is located on Chakphet Road. Taxi or river Express Boat to Saphan Phut station is the easiest way to get there.

There are other markets such as KlongToey Fresh Market, Bangkok Farmers Market, Pratunam Market and Dalat Rot Fai which worth a visit. These markets are vibrant places where once could experience the life of the city.

Sunday market

It is another important market in Chiang Mai city. This place has many handcrafter items and souvenirs for sale. The mask of Buddha is one of the famous items sold here. There is music, food and other means of entertainment to engage the crowd. These markets receive over 100,000 customers during the peak season.

Paragon Cineplex

Those looking for a comfortable cinema experience should go to the fifth floor of Siam Paragon. Upon incoming, visitors will be able to sport shinning ceilings, lighted staircases, and an extensive gourmet popcorn salesperson. The theater is a comfortable place to visit, and 4D movie is watched. To make the film incredible and memorable, the Paragon Cineplex has the largest screen.

Quartier Cine Art

It's one of the luxurious theaters. It usually displays the latest films produced by famous actors. The theaters have more deluxe equipped with pillows and plush recliners. They are always a hologram employee working out, and this is what makes the Quartier cinema to attract more visitors as it's well equipped with modern technology.

SF Cinema City

The most amazing things people love when visiting a movie is to meet overwhelming fresh popcorn. It has the appropriate show time that makes it suitable for anyone to come and watch the movie they want at any time of the day. Outside the theatre, it has numerous restaurants that offer better snacks and beverages to enjoy at a lower price. This theatre has a unique fun attraction that is located on the same floor including Escape room, Hero City Games Center and more.

House RCA

Those considering for many varieties of screenings should go to House RCA. It offers many movies such as independent films, blockbuster hits, Art films, international film, and award-winning film. It features videos within the world and cool cinema welcoming from places like Japan, China, Cambodia, Malaysia, and Italy.

Scala Theatre

Bangkok movie theaters are designed with the modern city vibe. Each new cinema has to be updated more attractively to attract more customers. The theater is more attractive as it contains golden flowers petals. It's the only movie show that takes back the views in the time of décor. This Scala Theatre is very fantastic as it's located in the modern areas within the city. It's always opened on a daily basis, and it's affordable for everyone.

Chainat Bird Park, Chainat

It's found in Central Thailand, and it's an enjoyable place to be. It's usually visited by adults and children who come to see a giant eagle sitting in the center of a small lake. It has a small water park that has bright slides that come out from the shiny colored robot. It has whimsical statues and egg museum where people come to learn more about its features.

The White Temple, Chiang Rai

One of Chiang Rai's most spectacular human-made places. It's one of the country most beautiful temples. It's ornamented with amusing artwork that usually attracts more visitors. Visitors can come with a camera to take amazing photos.

Bua Tong Waterfalls

This is located around 60 km away from the Chiang Mai city. A motorbike ride takes you here in 40 to 50 mins. Bua Tong waterfalls are beautiful and a pollution free area. One can go swinging in the river under the waterfall. This is a favorite Thai picnic place. Normally families go there.

Haad Pak Meng, Trang

The southern region of Trang is to some extent off the beaten track. While the island surely has the stars of the province, always create time to explore the mainland beach of Haad Pak Meng. It's a small a small distance from the heart town; the beach provides excellent views of the landscape. The sandy beach is also covered with thousands of twisty seashells.

Photography

Thailand is a gorgeous place to be, and with all your extra time, why not get the knowledge to capture its beauty. A visit along the beach, Hike Mountains, or tours through the night market will provide you with enough chance to take amazing photos of the landscape.

Kite surfing

It's one of the beach sport in Thailand. Hua Hin has a better school with inexpensive packages to teach people how the activity is done on the beach. It's always good for the new leaners who wish to participate in the game. Once you get the skills you can get your safety gear and head out at yourself, there is nothing better being on the wave, and you are stable.

Scuba diving

The island of Koh Tao is still the affordable places in the world to get PADI certified. There are many other islands which are a better place for beginners who want to dive in the deep. Once you have completed it, then I'm afraid you won't be able to stop. Your future holidays may be structured around it. It is a truly appreciated skill for one to have and there are always new things to explore.

Pai

It's one of the fantastic villages in Northern Thailand; it has a picture square valley and fresh atmosphere for any person to relax. Pai is a gorgeous place where many visitors wish to come and explore the area. It's situated around the foothills of the mountains and hills. It's also near the Pai city; they have fantastic hot springs, elephant camps, and amazing waterfalls. The Pai River offers turbine and remarkable adventures to visitors.

Phanom Rung

It's situated on the extinct volcano in Northeastern Thailand. It's one of the Hindus shrine buildings that is known for its outstanding architecture. This temple was constructed by Khmer culture in 10th to 13th centuries as the main dedication to Hindu god. It was built by use of latrine and sandstone that makes it appears fantastic. It was created to represent mount Kailash, which is the sacret of Shiva. It's better to place for any visitor to come to explore and take photos of the area.

Kanchanaburi

Situated in western Thailand and its visited by many people due to its fantastic scenery, and it's easy to get into the national park and waterfalls, Kanchanaburi is famously due to the Bridge above the River Kwai that was connected with the historical death of the prisoners who died during the world war II. It has museums and war cemeteries that always have information about the past event of the city and the building of the bridge in 1940 by Japan occupation. Outside the Kanchanaburi, there are fantastic parks such as Srinakarind and Erawan which have beautiful scenery, waterfalls, and caves. These features are the one that makes more visitors immerse themselves to come and explore.

Railay

Railay is a small peninsula in south Thailand that is only reachable by use of a boat due to the high limestone. Cliffs are the natural feature that usually attracts visitors from over the world. It has fantastic scenery, beaches, and cooling atmosphere for anyone to relax. For those who wish to come to this place, they should come to explore its environment and have a remarkable trip from Railay land.

Sathorn, Bangkok

It's a central and quiet neighborhood in Bangkok. It's located within the Chao Phraya River. It's a better place for any person to live because of its affordable price, its comfort, and its natural environment makes it a suitable place to live.

Koh Tao

It's one of the smallest islands, Koh Tao offers the best-laid back and authentic island for any person to live. Its community has invested in developing its infrastructure of the island. Tao prized is one of the most significant industries in which majority of people living in the island are employed to work in the hospitality industry.

Hua Hin

Hua Hin is extensively recognized as a capital residential holiday playground. It has become home for retiree experts who want to live golden years at a low price and better standards. The capital has better dining, market areas, beachside areas, and a home for golf courses in Thailand. This place is very calm and quite for any person to enjoy living.

Nimmanhaemin, Chiang Mai

Chiang Mai has encouraged experts to come and live in for many decades. The city offers low prizes to houses, and it's a convenient place to live. Nimman is the neighborhood of most local experts which has various accommodation facilities and better restaurant for any visitor.

Outdoor Adventures and Nature

Buddha Hill

This is one among the tallest points in Pattaya. At the top of the point lies the biggest statue of Buddha. Near this statue area is dedicated to Confucius and Lao-zi. Nearby this area another point is a monument which is dedicated to Kromluang Chomphonkhetudomsak who is the father of the Thai Navy.

Bridge on the River Kwai

This bridge is a historical place in Kanchanaburi. This was built with the forced labor of British, Dutch, and American prisoners of war during WWII. Many mainstream books were written on the context of the bridge. The bridge was part of the Thai-Burmese "Death Railway". The name was due to the fact that many men died during the construction of this bridge. Rides are available along the bridge and the bridge retains some of the parts from the original construction.

Three Pagodas Pass

It is recognized as a geographically important site in Thailand. It takes the name from Three Pagodas Faul. It is located about 250 km from Kanchanaburi. It basically marks the Thai-Burmese border which was a stop on ancient trade routes and also has a historical significance in ancient wars between Thailand and Burma. The pass and the surrounding areas are inhabited by the hill tribe communities which mainly consist of ethnic minority groups of Thai and/or Burmese origin. There are markets at the border. To enter Burma for tourist purposes the travelers must fly into the country and have a Burmese visa.

Erawan Waterfall

Erawan Waterfall is located at Northwest of Thailand. It's a home based to the well-known Erawan National Park. Erawan Waterfall runs through the east side of the national park and goes up to 1.5 km. Visitors can come with cameras to take amazing photos within its environment.

Khlong Lan Waterfall

The Khlong Lan Waterfall is one of the greatest waterfalls in Thailand. The waterfall is about 100 meters tall and 40 meters wide. This waterfall is located at Kamphaeng Phet province which is about 5 hours from North Bangkok.

Sridit Waterfall

AT North of Bangkok is where the Sridit Waterfall is located. The waterfall is a bit small, but it's the best place to have a leisure time by swimming and enjoying Thailand tropical heat. During the rainy season, Sridit waterfall is the best place to come and explore its amazing landscape scenery.

Mae Ya Waterfall

Mae Ya Waterfall is located at Chiang Mai. It's one of the tallest waterfalls in Thailand. It's about 260 meters height and 100 meters wide. It's an amazing place to visit because of its layered levels of the waterfall. When you visit this place ensure to come with a camera to take amazing photos.

Phliu Waterfall

Phliu Waterfall is positioned at Chanthaburi province. Near it, we have a great national park known as Namtok Phlio. It's a gorgeous place for one to visit in general and it's widely known over the world because of its waterfalls.it has many holes filled with fish and also visitors can enjoy the activity of swimming. All visitors are welcomed to the waterfall for a picnic.

Khlong Chak Waterfall

Khlong Chak Waterfall is located at the island of Koh Lanta.to reach to the waterfall; then you will have to pass through the elephant's sanctuaries and Monkeys Park that normally watch you from distance while passing. Khlong Chak Waterfall is usually dry during dry season. It's better if you visit the park during the rainy season and don't forget to carry a camera to take photos of the beautiful scenery.

Viking Cave, Koh Phi Phi Ley

It's one of the limestone caves. It has amazing drawings of ancient Viking ships on its wall. The cave is famously known to have a certain bird that is used in traditional Chinese soup. To get to this stunning cave, you will have to use a boat, and the cave is longer open to tourists.

Tham Lot, Pang Mapha

For any visitor to explore the cave there are two options; you are required to have a tour guide to give you the direction. The second option is to walk towards the bamboo raft then you will have to walk back through the forest. You will be required to be healthy as you will climb up and down the staircases exploring the caves highlights. They are various activities that one can participate in like kayaking and hiking hills.

Tham Chiang Dao, Chiang Dao

Chiang Dao is the best, and impressive limestone cave for one to come and explore.it has about 100 caves in the complex that occupies over 10km into the mountain. Inside the cave, we have statues, shrines, and Buddha images. It's better to take a tour guide if you want to go deeper into the cave and you will have to pay a small entrance fee.

Phraya Nakhon Cave

The cave is situated at Hua Hin which is about 45 minutes' drive. It's one of the most beautiful caves in Thailand. Traveling to the cave, you will have to go through rugged mountains, lush forest, and past white sand beaches. The cave has two chambers that allow sunlight to stream into the cave. The main cave chamber is at Kuha Karuhas Pavilion which is a magical sight to explore.

Monkey Cave (Wat Tham Suwan Khuha Cave Temple)

The cave has many monkeys jumping up and down within the cave, so visitors are urged to be more careful in the cave. The cave has an amazing gold Buddha statue that normally attracts tourists. The cave has plenty of light with big room, and it's the best for those people who get claustrophobic in tight space.

Thale Noi Lake

Thale Noi is one of the best beautiful natural lakes in Thailand. The lake is covered with millions of white water lilies and pink that normally have a vibrant golden stem. Visitors are also attracted to come and birdwatch of beautiful birds such as cotton geese and herons. In February and April is the best time for visitors to come to birdwatch.

Nong Han Lake

The lake Nong Han is located along the Phu Phan Yon N national Park. The lake is very deep, and visitors are urged to be very careful when exploring the lake. The lake is surrounded by beautiful hills making it appear more attractive and amazing. Visitors are allowed to come with a camera to take photos within the lake environment.

Bueng Boraphet

Bung Boraphet is one of the tourist attraction lakes. It's one of the largest fresh water lakes in Thailand. The Lake has amazing statue still water ornamented with lush immersed foliage. The lake covers about 200 square kilometers. This lake is a habitat for many animals, and plants.vistors can use the boat to explore the lake, and they should be accompanied with a tour guide to give them direction.

Pang Ung Lake

The Pang Ung Lake is one of the remarkable lakes for any visitor to come and explore. The lake is surrounded by a mountain and forest that makes it to be a quiet environment for visitors to relax. It's a perfect place for those with a passion for exploring natural resources in Thailand. The lake is home to many animals and plants. Around the lake we have simple homestays and accommodation where visitors can sleep and have food.

Kwan Phayao

The lake is one of the largest lakes in Thailand, and it's very beautiful due to the surrounding mountain and temple. The lake is a home based to many plants and animals that stay in the water. The lake is believed to have stayed over 500 years, and it was created in 1939 to improve irrigation on the firms.

Queen Sirikit Botanic Garden

The Queen Sirikit Botanic Garden is one of the most well-known gardens in Thailand. It's a suitable place to carry out scientific research by students and scientists. Visitors can also explore amazing palms and orchids while roaming around the beautiful grounds. The garden is mostly visited in the morning hours at around 8:30 am.

Royal Park Rajapruek

The Ratchaphruek Flower Gardens is located at Chiang Mai area. The garden is incredible and picturesque. To travel to the garden, you can use the electric bus or rental bikes that can take you around the garden. The garden is mostly opened between 8 am to 6 pm after which it is closed.

Tweechol Botanic Garden

The garden is very fantastic since workers usually maintain it in the morning hours. The garden is immaculate for anyone to spend a day inside. The garden has numerous trees, lovely Topiaries and flowers. It also has an orchid area and a tropical place that has a herb garden, fish pond, and cactuses flowers.

Bann Phor Liang Meun

This garden has full of greeneries and sculptures. The garden has a beautiful temple inside. Most of the visitors usually come to rest and drink beverages. This place is perfect for one to visit. It has a cooling environment and fresh air that makes it an exciting place to visit. Visitors can carry their camera to take wonderful photos of the garden.

Krabi

Krabi is famously known to be an area for rock climbers who normally come to climb the big stones. There are enough packages available. Those who wish to climb the stones are requested to come with protective gear to wear. It has better cliffs which are suitable for climbers.

Aow Leuk Beach, Koh Tao

Koh Tao is one of the best places to carry out snorkeling. It's positioned at Southwest coast. Many snorkelers usually put on their safety gear before diving into the lake. Its coral reefs are relatively shallow.

TOP 10 Beaches

Thailand has one of the most attractive and cooling beaches for tourists to visit. These are the best beaches for any tourist to come to explore during the holiday season.

Pattaya Beach

A three-kilometer long beach is the major attraction of the city. There are plenty of hotels, restaurants and shopping centers by the beaches here. The beer bars and go-go's are another attraction. Thai massage centers are dotted throughout the area. The Pattaya beach is followed by several small beaches; some of these beaches have restricted access.

West KoPha Nagn

West KoPha Nagn is one of the famous beaches. The travelers can rent small boats to explore other parts of the island. There are more activities organized on the beach during the day. The beach gives a wonderful view of the sunset. After the sunset one could go to beer bars to relax.

Khao Lak

Khao Lak is one of the amazing beaches in Thailand. It offers a better remote vacation for people to relax. Near the beach, it's uninhabited with lush rainforest and wildlife that attracts tourists from over the world. The beach offers various activities such as scuba and fishing. During December and November, the water at the beach is usually warm.

Phuket Thailand Beach

March and November, the beach is often crowded with visitors from over the world. The beach offers exciting activities like scuba diving, sunbathing, and swimming. It has attraction landscape near the beach that one can go to explore. It contains warm and clear water that attracts visitors to come to enjoy and relax on its cooling environment.

Phi Phi Don Thailand beach

It's mostly known to be a well-known beach in entire Thailand. This beach offers a gratifying activity like breathtaking and sun basking on the warm sand of the beach. November and December, it's usually crowded with children and adults who come to have leisure time on the beach.

West Railay Thailand beach

If you want cooling and quiet environment to enjoy the holiday, then the West Railay is the best beach to be. The water is very clear, and the beach contains milky white sand. It offers incredible activities like fishing and scuba diving. For any visitor to come to this beach, then they will have to use a boat.

Ao Nang Beach

The Ao Nang Beach is mostly crowded mostly on holiday. It attracts several tourists with its beautiful scenery around. When you are around the beach, you will spot Krabi limestone that is visible. It's highly developed, and there is no need to take a boat to reach the beach, it has small shops that tourist immerse themselves to buy food and beautiful products. Ao Nang has various water sports such as jungle zip line and diving.

Haad Rin Beach

This beach is famously due to its amazing full party moon, and it's situated on the island of Ko Phangan. The entire moon party attracts more visitors who typically come to the beach. During this party, the beach is lined up with the big sound system and crowded with visitors who come to the party. Most parties are held at night hours on the beach and streets of Haad Rin. The beach offers unusual activities such as sun basking on the sand, swimming, and diving.

Lamai Beach

Lamai Beach is situated in Samui. Visitors who are looking for a resort place will enjoy Lamai Beach. Lamai beach is a quiet resort to visit. It's smaller in size, and it tends to be less crowded. Lamai beach has the best white sand which is appropriate for visitors to relax. The beach has various restaurants, bars, and activities to keep visitors busy.

White Sand Beach, Koh Chang

It's one of the best resort scene beaches for one to come to visit. It has many resorts and evening buffets that occupies the beach. As the name of the beach implies, it is covered with soft, white, and powdery sand that attracts people to come and lay on it. Along the beach, it's occupied with coconut trees and palm. The beach offers many activities such as swimming, sand bathing, and diving.

Kata Beach, Phuket

Kata Beach is one of the most refreshing and more relaxed beaches in the Southern Phuket. Kata is a favorite because of its warm water, amazing scenery, and palm trees surrounding the beach. The beach has gorgeous resorts, hotels, and shopping malls that offer a variety of products to visitors. Tourists can enjoy a number of activities like snorkeling, surfing, and boogie boarding.

Patong Beach

Visitors who love basking on the sun during the day, then Patong Beach is the appropriate place to be. The beach is surrounded with vibrant restaurants, tourists' shops, bars, and nightclubs. This beach offers activities such as snorkeling, diving, and surfing.

Hat Pramong

Sunset Beach, which is situated on a small bay on Ko Lipe, also known as the Hat Pramong. As the name suggests, this beach is positioned on the west and offers spectacular sunsets. It's a quiet, and gorgeous beach that will provide visitors with a glimpse of the way Thailand used to look out. Currently, Sunset Beach is not yet home to great resorts. Visitors can appreciate the simple life in comfortable bungalows and huts.

Sairee Beach

Sairee beach is situated on the west side; it offers one of the best activities such as scuba divers and snorkelers for visitors to enjoy and have a marvelous trip from the beach. The beach nearby is a bit relatively crucial low area, but still, it has nightclubs and bars that offer a sweet cocktail table to the visitors. You can reach the Sairee Beach by either using a ferry service or by use of aircraft.

Eat and Drink

Thailand is extensively identified over the world for its mouthwatering cuisine and delicate balance of salty, spicy, sweet, and bitter flavors.

Guay Teow

Guay Teow is one of the delicious meals in Thailand. Pork, beef, and chicken are usually used to prepare Guay Teow. It's advisable to add egg noodles and rice noodles. Most cookers frequently add wontons and meatballs to the broth when cooking. Guy Teow meal is topped with a variety of condiments such as lime juice, fish sauce, dried chili peppers, and sugar. It can be served at any time of the day.

Tom Kha Gai

Tom Kha Gai is linked to tom yum, and it makes people enjoy its delicious taste with better flavors as well as spice scale. Tom Kha Gai is usually made with a variety of ingredients such as creamy coconut milk. Most of the vegetables enjoyed by people in Thailand are easily malleable. This food is very delicious when served at lunchtime.

Laab

Laab is a meal that originated in the North Eastern province of Isan. The meal contains mushrooms, meat, and salad. Laab is cooked with many ingredients like pork, mushroom, and chicken. It's not suitable for those people whose bodies can't be in a position to regulate the number of spices since the meal has a high percentage of spices. This food is rich in protein, and is suitable for bodybuilding.

Pad Krapow

Pad krapow is frequently cooked using chicken and minced pork. It's then stirred with chilies and Thai basil. Thai basil contains high, peppery taste, while chilies add a high amount of spices in the meal. This meal is served with topped egg and white rice. It's very delicious, and it has proteins and carbohydrates that are appropriate for the use of body development. It is usually served in the lunchtime hours.

Gaeng Keow Wan (Green Curry)

Gaeng Keow Wan food originated in central Thailand. Green curry is the spiciest food with a sweet taste from the added coconut milk. Green Curry is made from one of the best mouthwatering ingredients such as ginger, fresh green chilies, eggplant, and plenty of coconut milk. It's worthwhile to enjoy the food with steamed rice to decrease the spice level in the Gaeng Keow Wan food.

Gai Tod (Fried Chicken)

Gai Tod is tremendously known in Thailand. Gai Tod is usually cooked by marinating drumsticks or chicken wings in a blend of spices and rice flour. For the chicken to be delicious, then it's served by spicy sauce like nam jim. Use of sticky rice usually eats Gai Tod, and it makes it the best food one has to eat when he/she visit Thailand.

Park Boong (Morning Glory)

Park boong is a very healthy food for any visitor to eat in Thailand. This spinach vegetable is usually fried and seasoned with soy sauce, garlic, chilies, and soybean paste. Park boong is spicy, sauce, salty and crunchy, satisfying anybody palette. Park Boong is often created with oysters' sauce.

Som Tam (Spicy Green Papaya Salad)

Som Tam is one of the delicious food in Northeastern Thailand. Som tam contains a variety of ingredients such as carrots, tomatoes, dried shrimp, runner beans, green papaya, peanuts, lime juice, palm sugar, and tamarind pulp. Pestle and mortar are used to mix the ingredients. This food contains proteins and vitamins that are essential to the development of the body.

Yam Talay (Spicy Seafood Salad)

It's a mixture of seafood salad, and it's one of the most delicious food in Thailand. It's essential and healthy for the body as it has vital nutrients that are required by the body for growth. This salad has various components such as mussels, squid, shrimp, and scallops in it. To increase the flavor of the Yaam Talay many ingredients are added like tomatoes, onions, and a glass of rice.

Pad See Ew (Thick Noodle Dish)

Pad See Ew contains rice noodles which are fried in a sauce with pork, Chinese broccoli, cabbage, beef, and chicken. When cooked well it's very delicious and safe food for those people whose body can't be able to control spicier level in the body. Chilli flakes and vinegar can be added to increase its flavor. This food is worthy as it has a high percentage of proteins and vitamins in it.

Sugarcane Juice

This drink is delightful. Due to its sweetness then it's not possible to leave Thailand without taking a bottle of juice. This juice can be found at any vendor shop at the affordable price, and it's manufactured with high standards by use of powerful machines.

Thai beer

Alcoholic drinks are sweet to enjoy on weekends to remove stress. These drinks are affordable at a lower price and easy accessibility. Singa and Chang beers are famous brands which are renowned in Thailand due to its sweet and fantastic taste. You can purchase them at any convenient store in the Thailand city.

Grass Jelly Drinks

All people in Thailand loves drinking grass jelly. Black jelly is created by mixing both ice and water before sprinkled it with brown sugar. Grass jelly can be added to things such as coconut ice cream, but the best way is to ingest it in beverages. Before adding a drink of your choice, jelly cubes are sliced and put inside the plastic cubes.

Coconut Water

Thick slices of coconuts are shaved out of its hard covering and mixed with water. You can add little sugar to add its flavor. Most vendors' usually make it and put it in a cylinder container from there it is scoped into a cup for visitors or for any customer to enjoy the drink.

Coffee

Thailand has many varieties of coffee to enjoy. We have many stalls selling coffee in Thailand at a suitable prize. These stalls usually sell different kinds of coffee including mochas and lattes. Always ensure to buy a barista since it looks to be one of the favorite drink in Thailand. This coffee can be found in coffee shops in urban areas of Thailand.

Thai Iced Milk Tea

Chai yen is one of the delicious drinks in Thailand; during morning hours is when it's served. The drink is orange in color. The tea is created by the combination of evaporated milk and condensed milk. It's rich in calcium that causes the bones to be healthy.

Smoothies

Most of these smoothies are made for the good benefits they bring, for example, you can buy orange, apple and pineapple smoothies to assist your body in the digestion system. A number of smoothies are made from watermelon by freshly blending and adding such ingredients like dragon fruits, carrots and more for flavor.

Pomegranate Juice

Thailand has many varieties of juices to drink, but pomegranate juice is the best to drink. Pomegranate juice is an essential juice in the body since it contains vitamin C and is packed with antioxidants and fiber. Thailand drinks generally have a lot of sugar that makes them more delightful for people to enjoy.

Thai whiskey

Mekhong and Songsom are the great drinks that are enjoyed by people in Thailand. It's because they are affordable to buy, making many people buy the drink. Thailand whiskeys are created from 95% molasses and sugarcane and five percent of rice. Since we have many drinks, people are advised to be very careful when taking the drinks since some of them are harmful to the body.

Nom Yen (iced milk with syrup)

Nom Yen is mostly used by children, teenagers, and those people who don't drink any variety of caffeine drinks. It's made from fresh hot milk which is mixed with red or green syrup. After that, it's mixed with ice. It can be consumed with steamed bread and coconut jam. Nom Yen can be found at the street shops of Thailand at a lower price.

TOP 10 Party Bars and Clubs

Onyx

Location: Royal City Avenue (RCA ซอยศูนย์วิจัย Thanon Phra Ram 9, Bang Kapi, Huai Khwang, Bangkok 10310

Onyx is one of the famous clubs in Thailand. It's a wonderful place for partying with friends and family. Onyx club is one of the biggest clubs in Thailand; it has a better dancing floor, high stools, and standing tables, the club also has an impressively cool Led screen that is placed behind the main DJ booth. Entrance fee to the club is inexpensive of about 400 to 500 baht. The club offers better cocktail drinks to the customers.

Insanity

Location: 32/2 Sukhumvit Rd, Khwaeng Khlong Toei Nuea, Khet Watthana, Krung Thep Maha Nakhon 10110

The club has many attractive features such as big room EDM, bass-heavy tunes, and Electro House Seven nights. The club gives the impression to be an international club, and it has the best local DJ'S. The club is usually fully occupied on the weekend, but it's also opened on weekdays. It's one of the biggest clubs with a retractable halo lighting system and Acoustic sound system. It has a better dancing floor, and it offers better drinks to the customers.

Sing Sing Theater

Location: ถนน สุขุมวิท ซอย สุขุมวิท 45 แขวง คลองเตย Khet Watthana, กรุงเทพมหานคร 10110

It's one of the best clubs with an interior design that usually attracts many people. The music played in this club at a high volume, and it's more ambitious than any other clubs in Thailand. These clubs provide elaborate entertainment to its customers. The club is truly unique, and it has elegant girls dressed in Chinese Qipao. The club is fully packed on weekends, and it's very affordable for all people.

Levels Club & Lounge

Location: Aloft Hotel 35 ถนน สุขุมวิท ซอย 11 Khlong Tan Nuea, Khet Watthana, Krung Thep Maha Nakhon 10110

This club is the cheapest one because you don't have to pay an entrance fee. It attracts most of the clubbers at night of the week. It usually conducts essential events on Friday and Wednesday. The club has better seating that offers a better environment for mingling with new friends. The club has a rooftop lounge and two club rooms. The Dj mostly plays Hip Hop song on the stage. It has a dancing floor and a high-quality sound system. It offers better cocktail drinks to its customers at a lower price.

Beam

Location: 72 Sukhumvit 55 Thonglor Khwaeng Khlong Tan Nuea, Khet Watthana, Krung Thep Maha Nakhon 10110

The club has fantastic sound systems including huge speakers. It has a Void Acoustics sound system. The club has a music policy which regulates the type of music played in the club. It has a downstairs which is packed with hip-hop fans. The club operates daily, and it offers cocktail drinks to the customers at a lower price.

DJ Station

Location: 11 Silom 2/1, Silom, Khet Bang Rak, Krung Thep Maha Nakhon 10500

It's one of the nightclub to visit. It's well known in Thailand as it's one of the legendary dance clubs. It's known to be one of the largest gay clubs in Thailand. The club has three different rooms to choose from; each housing has its club. The club usually conducts night shows which generally starts at around 11: 30 pm. It has one of the best DJs, and regardless of your gender, this is the best club to be to enjoy your leisure time with new friends.

Route 66

Location: 29/33 - 48 พระราม 9 ซอย ศูนย์วิจัย Khwaeng Bang Kapi, Khet Huai Khwang, Krung Thep Maha Nakhon 10310

People can come to Route 66 for the food or enjoy cocktails drinks that are offered. This club is positioned at Royal City Avenue. The entire area is commonly known to be an official nightlife zone. These clubs attract many crowds on weekends due to its massive venue, and best hip-hop music played in the club. It has live play music and Thai pop music to the fans. It's the best club to be as its cheap and a safe place.

Sugar club

Location: 37 Soi Sukhumvit 1/1, Khwaeng Khlong Toei Nuea, Khet Watthana, Krung Thep Maha Nakhon 10110

Sugar club plays hip-hop music typically. The Sugar club is positioned at infamous Soi 11. It's one of the best nightclubs in Thailand. The club is unique since it doesn't have a cocktail table and it's opened explicitly at 10 pm on the weekend and 11 pm during the weekdays. The club has the dancing floor and best Dj who plays the music for the fans.

Ce La Vi (Formerly Ku De Ta)

Location: Sathorn Square Tower N Sathon Rd, Khwaeng Silom, Khet Bang Rak, Krung Thep Maha Nakhon 10500

It's one of the top clubs that has never been opened in Thailand. The club has a sophisticated space with a rooftop. Music is played and changed according to the night event, most music that is played here is hip-hop songs on Wednesdays, the R'n'B music is played on Fridays with more bass heavy. It's appropriate if people dress nicely to impress people from the party. The club is usually crowded, and it's better to come early to get a sit.

Live RCA

Location: 94, 23/92-94 RCA Alley, Bangkok 10310

Live RCA club is one of the newest additions clubs in Thailand. It's located on the main party streets of Royal City Avenue. Live RCA usually plays life dance music to its fans, and it has international DJs who control the music at the stage. The club has an impressive sound system and LED light that makes it a good looking club. It has a large dancing floor that is usually fully occupied during important events on weekends.

Demo club

Location: 225/9 ซอยทองหล่อ 10 ถนนสุขุมวิท 55 Khlong Tan Nuea, Watthana, Bangkok 10110

Demo club is right located at the center of Bangkok high society on Thong Lor Street. It's fully crowded on Wednesday and Sundays. It offers sweet cocktails drinks to its customers. The club usually plays various kinds of music, and it has a dancing floor for fans to dance and enjoy themselves.

GLOW

Location: 96/4 ถนน สุขุมวิท ซอย 23 Khwaeng Khlong Toei Nuea, Khet Watthana, Krung Thep Maha Nakhon 10110

It's one of the best dance music clubs in Thailand. The club has two venues, but all activities are done downstairs on the small dancing floor. It has one of the experienced DJs who entertains the crowd with excellent music. The entrance fee to the club is about 200 to 500 baht, and you will get free cocktail drinks. On Friday and Saturday is when the club is jam-packed.

Original Local/Authentic Souvenirs

When you visit Thailand, it's good to buy unique products to take back home. Visitors are advised to immerse themselves in the street markets of Thailand since they have a variety of impressive products, food, textiles, and ornaments for one to buy. These are the best souvenirs that one can buy in Thailand.

Thai Silk

It's one of the most loved products by Thailand people, and you must buy it when you get to Thailand. It has beautiful colorful scarves, bags and fabric. There are many varieties of silks that one can buy. Jim Thompson House in Bangkok is the excellent place to buy a high-quality Thai Silk.

Thai Spa Products

It's fantastic to buy Thai Spa products to take them back home. You'll get a variety of scented candles, coconut oils, and domestic plant oil to buy which are very essentials to the body. It's also better to buy body scrubs; foot soaks and carved soaps which are the stunning products to take home.

Handmade Thai Jewelry

Thailand is one of the great nations to find unique jewelry to buy. Chiang Mai is well known to be a great shop where one can get a variety of high-quality bracelets, necklaces, gleaming cups, and plates. It's better to be cautious when buying jewelry of great value to avoid purchasing fake jewelry in the market.

Ceramics and Pottery

Thailand has one of the great artisans who make various types of ceramics and pottery. Bencharong porcelain and Sangkhalok are the most famous ceramics for one to buy in Thailand. Chiang Mai is a region with many factories that specialize in the making of pottery products and ceramics.

Wooden Furniture and Carvings

Many Ornate wooden furnishings and carvings are made from teak and are always available in Thailand. If visitors get at Chiang Mai, which is also known as furniture city, they will get many shops that sell furniture products, and all the shops will help them for international shipping if they procure one of the furniture.

Wickerwork

All types of wickerwork products can be procured in Thailand. It has a variety of products such as picture frames, furnishings, and hats coasters. Thai work products are created by using many products such as bulrush, bamboo, and rattan. Procure wickerwork in any shop and departments stores in the Thailand city.

Antiques

Antique products are the best to buy when it comes to Thailand. They are various antique products to buy such as fantastic silverware, woodcarvings, and pottery which are unique and of high quality. They are available in the shops at a lower price.

Elephants as Souvenirs

It's one of the great souvenirs to take home, and the elephant is a symbol of Thailand country. It's better if you procure a product with an elephant on it such as chocolate elephants, ornaments, paintings, colorful bag, and wood carvings that has an elephant image on it. All these products can be procured at any Thailand shop.

Thai Sauces and Spices

Thailand has delicious foods that one can buy and come with it at homes such as sauces, herbs, and spices. When you buy one of the packets of sauces or spices then is an excellent souvenir one has to take home. You can get great commercially pack spices and sauces which are free from taxes making them affordable to buy.

Tuk-tuk Ornaments

Another well-known Thai symbol is the tuk-tuk. Decide to procure one and take it home as miniature as a great way to remember memories of your tuk-tuk travels in Thailand.

Thai Alcohol

Thailand Alcohol is very expensive because of the taxes imposed on selling them. The alcohol is very sweet, and most people are advised to procure Chang beer, Singha beer, and Som Whiskey to take home to enjoy with friends and relatives.

Muay-Thai Shorts

These Thailand shorts are stunning and of high quality. Most of the shorts are for the Muay Thai boxing class. It's better to buy them to be always reminding you of the best trip you had in Thailand.

Thai Loincloths

These interesting patterned pieces of fabric are crated from cotton and silk. They have stayed part of the Thai wardrobe since earliest times and are very versatile. They are tremendous and good-looking souvenir for one to take home.

Printed in Great Britain
by Amazon